W9-BED-491

THE CITY

LIFE IN THE ROMAN EMPIRE
THE CITY

BY

KATHRYN HINDS

BENCHMARK BOOKS

MARSHALL CAVENDISH
NEW YORK

To the wonderful teachers of Lumpkin County Middle School

The author and publisher wish to specially thank J. Brett McClain
of the Oriental Institute of the University of Chicago
for his invaluable help in reading the manuscript.

❧

Benchmark Books   Marshall Cavendish   99 White Plains Road   Tarrytown, New York 10591-9001
www.marshallcavendish.com   Copyright © 2005 by Marshall Cavendish Corporation   All rights
reserved. No part of this book may be reproduced or utilized in any form or by any means electronic
or mechanical including photocopying, recording, or by any information storage and retrieval system, without permission from the copyright holders.   All Internet sites were available and accurate
when this book was sent to press.   Book design by Michael Nelson   LIBRARY OF CONGRESS
CATALOGING-IN-PUBLICATION DATA: Hinds, Kathryn, 1962-   The city / Kathryn Hinds.   p. cm.
— (Life in the Roman empire)   Includes bibliographical references and index.   ISBN 0-7614-1655-2
1. Rome—Social life and customs—Juvenile literature. 2. City and town life—Rome—Juvenile literature.
I. Title II. Series: Hinds, Kathryn, 1962- . Life in the Roman empire.   DG78.H55 2005   937'.6—
dc22   2004008255

Art Research: Rose Corbett Gordon, Mystic CT
Front cover: Galerie Daniel Greiner, Paris/Archives Charmet/Bridgeman Art Library. Back cover: The
Art Archive/Museo della Civilta Romana Rome/Dagli Orti. Pages i, 22, 40, 61, 65: Scala/Art Resource,
NY;   page iii: Gilles Mermet/Art Resource, NY;   page vi: Chedworth Roman Villa, Gloucestershire,
UK/National Trust Photographic Library/Ian Shaw/Bridgeman Art Library;   pages viii, 68: Museo
della Civilta Romana, Rome/Giraudon/ Bridgeman Art Library;   page 3: Private Collection/Christo-
pher Wood Gallery, London/Bridgeman Art Library;   page 4: Giraudon/Art Resource, NY;   page 5:
Verulamium Museum, St.Albans, Hertfordshire, UK/Bridgeman Art Library;   pages 7, 11: The
Granger Collection, New York;   pages 8, 15: Roger Wood/Corbis;   page13: Phillips, The International
Fine Art Auctioneers, UK/Bridgeman Art Library;   pages 14, 18, 46: Mimmo Jodice/Corbis;   pages 17,
28, 64, 77: Araldo de Luca/Corbis;   page19: Gustavo Tomsich/Corbis;   pages 20, 39: Werner For-
man/Art Resource, NY;   page 21: Archivo Iconografico, S.A./Corbis;   pages 24, 25, 50, 54: Erich
Lessing/Art Resource, NY;   page 27: Museo della Civilta Romana, Rome/ Bridgeman Art Library; page
29: Musée des Antiquités Nationales, St- Germain-en-Laye, France/Lauros/Giraudon/ Bridgeman Art
Library;   page 32: The Art Archive/Museo della Civilta Romana Rome/Dagli Orti;   page 37: Louvre,
Paris/Lauros/Giraudon/ Bridgeman Art Library;   page 42: Villa dei Misteri, Pompeii, Italy/ Bridgeman
Art Library;   page 44: The Art Archive / Museo Nazionale Terme Rome / Dagli Orti;   page 47: Ali-
nari/Art Resource, NY;   page 48: Sandro Vannini/Corbis;   page 53: The Art Archive/Museo della
Civilta Romana, Rome/Dagli Orti;   page 56: The Art Archive/Archaeological Museum Salonica/Dagli
Orti;   page 58: Christie's Images/Corbis;   page 63: Hulton Archive/Getty Images;   page 71: SEF/Art
Resource, NY;   page 72: Roger Ressmeyer/Corbis.

Printed in China
1 3 5 6 4 2

front cover: Part of the Roman Forum, imagined by a modern artist
back cover: Children at play, from the port city of Ostia
half-title page: A portrait of a baker and his wife from Pompeii
title page: Part of a mosaic from a home in Roman-ruled North Africa
About the Roman Empire, p. vi: A personification of Spring, from a mosaic found on the floor of a dining
room in Britain

CONTENTS

✧

✧

ABOUT THE ROMAN EMPIRE

When we think about the Roman Empire, we often picture gladiators, chariot races, togas, marble statues, and legions on the march. These images tell only part of the story of ancient Rome. According to the Romans themselves, their city was founded in 753 B.C.E.* At first Rome was ruled by kings, then it became a republic. In 27 B.C.E. Augustus Caesar became Rome's absolute ruler—its first emperor. Meanwhile, this city built on seven hills overlooking the Tiber River had been steadily expanding its power. In Augustus's time Rome controlled all of Italy and the rest of mainland Europe west of the Rhine River and south of the Danube River, as well as much of North Africa and the Middle East.

At its height the Roman Empire reached all the way from Britain to Persia. It brought together an array of peoples on three continents, forming a vibrant multicultural society. During much of the empire's existence, its various ethnic and religious groups got along with remarkable tolerance and understanding—a model that can still inspire us today. We can also be inspired by the Romans' tremendous achievements in the arts, architecture, literature, law, and philosophy, just as they have inspired and influenced people in Europe and the Americas for hundreds of years.

So step back in time, and visit Rome at its most powerful, from 27 B.C.E. to around 200 C.E., the first two centuries of the empire. In this book you will meet craftsmen, merchants, slaves, soldiers, and other residents of Roman cities. These people had many of the same joys and sorrows, hopes and fears that we do, but their world was very different from ours. Forget about telephones, computers, cars, and televisions, and imagine what it might have been like to live among the people who ruled much of the ancient world. Welcome to life in the Roman Empire. . . .

* A variety of systems of dating have been used by different cultures throughout history. Many historians now prefer to use B.C.E (Before Common Era) and C.E. (Common Era) instead of B.C. (Before Christ) and A.D. (Anno Domini), out of respect for the diversity of the world's peoples. In this book, all dates are C.E. unless otherwise noted.

AN EMPIRE OF CITIES

EVEN NOW, I SEE A CITY . . . GREATER THAN ANY OTHER THAT IS OR
WILL BE OR WAS SEEN IN AGES PAST.
—OVID, *METAMORPHOSES*

ccording to legend, Rome began with a collection of shepherds, escaped slaves, and men looking for a new start in life. Archaeologists have recently proven that during the eighth century B.C.E., the early Romans—whoever they were—definitely organized themselves and founded a city. Over the next few centuries, as history tells us, Rome expanded its rule to nearby cities and the rural areas they controlled.

Many of Rome's neighbors had a similar culture and spoke the same language, Latin, as the Romans. Other peoples of the area, such as the Etruscans, were quite different. Rome conquered them all, sometimes absorbing aspects of the conquered societies, but always imposing its own language, laws, and government.

opposite: Many cities in the Roman Empire began as military bases, like the one at which these soldiers are working.

1

As Rome's territory grew, so did the variety of cultures it incorporated. Southern Italy had many Greek settlements; northern Italy was the home of Celtic tribes (related to the Welsh and Irish of today). Outside of Italy, the Romans took over numerous well-established cities in eastern and southern regions such as Greece, Syria, and Egypt. There were far fewer urban areas in northwestern Europe. Where the Romans did not find cities, however, they created them. The Roman Empire embraced many languages and cultures, but all of the provinces under Roman rule came to have at least one thing in common: the importance of cities.

THE NETWORK OF POWER

"Goddess of continents and peoples, O Rome, whom nothing can equal and nothing approach"—this was how the Spanish-born poet Martial addressed the city he had adopted as his home. His feelings were shared by many. Rome was the largest and most powerful city in the western world. It was not only the capital of the empire, but was also a center of religion, literature, and culture. And it was home to more than a million people, a huge population for ancient times.

Rome reached its supreme status largely because of the great discipline, skill, and efficiency of the Roman army, for as the army won more territory, the city had more resources available to it. The Roman talent for organizing and engineering went hand in hand with this military might. When the soldiers of the Roman legions were not fighting, they were often at work on building projects, such as roads. These roads, in turn, made it easy for the legions, stationed throughout the empire, to receive supplies and deploy to trouble spots.

The impressive network of paved roads that connected the capital with the rest of the empire was not just for military use. Messengers to and from the emperor traveled with government communications. Students and tourists paid visits to the empire's great centers of learning and other famous sites. Merchants journeyed the roads with their carts and pack trains, loaded with olive oil, wine, cloth, produce, building materials, and other goods destined for the great city.

The Tiber River was another kind of roadway, linking Rome with the Mediterranean. From the port city of Ostia, barges made the twenty-mile trip upriver to Rome bearing a world of luxurious imports: silk and spices from the East, marble and works of art from Greece and Asia Minor, pearls and rare purple dye from Syria, linen and glass from Egypt. The most important cargo of all, however, was grain, shipped from Sicily and North Africa: more than six million sacks of grain a year were required to feed the people of the city of Rome.

A nineteenth-century artist's view of the Roman Forum, the city's center. In the foreground is the Arch of Septimius Severus; in the background, near the center, is the Colosseum.

AN EMPIRE OF CITIES

3

Magnificent feats of Roman engineering, aqueducts were built all over the empire. This one can still be seen near Segovia, Spain.

A sure food supply was one of Rome's greatest needs. Equally important was the water supply. Roman engineering guaranteed that fresh water was plentiful—in the amount of some 250 million gallons a day. Eleven aqueducts brought this precious resource to the city from rivers and springs in the hills to the south and east. The water flowed in underground conduits or covered trenches for much of the way. To cross gorges and rivers, the conduits were laid over bridges supported by soaring arches. A water commissioner in 97 C.E. expressed the Romans' pride in these marvels of practical engineering in this way: "Will anybody compare the idle pyramids, or those other useless though renowned works of the Greeks with these aqueducts, these many indispensable structures?"

EXPORTING URBAN LIFE

Rome became the pattern for other cities in the empire. This was not so surprising in Italy, where generations of sharing a common culture naturally resulted in similar styles of building and urban development. Elsewhere, however, the Romans very deliberately promoted their own kind of urban lifestyle. For example, after southern Britain was conquered in the middle of the first century,

Roman governors encouraged the native people to abandon their scattered rural settlements. The historian Tacitus described how his father-in-law, Agricola, governor of Britain for a number of years, used "the charms of luxury" to persuade his subjects to stop fighting the Romans and embrace city-based Roman ways:

> Agricola gave private encouragement and public aid to the building of temples, courts of justice and dwelling-houses, praising the energetic, and reproving the indolent [lazy]. . . . He likewise provided a liberal education for the sons of the chiefs. . . . [T]hey who lately disdained the tongue of Rome now coveted its eloquence. Hence, too, a liking sprang up for our style of dress, and the "toga" became fashionable. Step by step they [the British people] were led to things which dispose to vice, the lounge, the bath, the elegant banquet. All this in their ignorance, they called civilization, when it was but a part of their servitude.

This reconstruction of a temple in second-century Britain shows a combination of native and Roman building styles.

Where the Romans didn't have to build new cities, they often renovated and expanded existing ones. Emperors or wealthy citizens financed the construction of Roman-style temples, public buildings, marketplaces, bathhouses, monuments, and theaters in the cities of Greece, Asia Minor, and North Africa. Roman benefactors also frequently improved water supplies (by building aqueducts), harbor facilities, and the like. Such actions earned the gratitude of the cities' leading citizens, who were happy to enjoy these benefits of Roman rule.

By the second century the Mediterranean world was dotted with "little Romes," cities whose architecture, language, money, and laws all expressed their belonging to the empire. A person from a city in Gaul (France) could visit a city in what is now western Turkey, more than two thousand miles away overland, and feel almost perfectly at home. Everyone paid for things with the same selection of silver, brass, and bronze coins; nearly everyone spoke either Latin or Greek. The surroundings were familiar: here would be the city center with its markets, law courts, and statues of the emperors; here were the temples dedicated to the deities that were worshipped all over the Roman world; here was an aqueduct supplying bathhouses and fountains.

The Romans called this cultural, political, and economic unity *pax Romana*, usually translated as "the Roman peace." But in the ancient world, *pax* meant not only a state of harmony, but, more importantly, one of order, where everything worked according to "the rules"—that is, the Romans' rules.

THE ARMY'S ROLE

The Roman army played a major part in developing urban life throughout the empire. The army's first role in this process was of

～⚬ CITIES GREAT AND SMALL ⚬～

I used to think the city men call Rome
Was like our market-town, to which we come
On market days, and drive our kids to sell.
O foolishness. . . .

The great Roman poet Virgil put those words into the mouth of a shepherd in northern Italy. It's no wonder that this country dweller was stupefied when he saw how much larger Rome was than the small town he visited on market day, for the imperial capital was home to more than a million people.

The next largest cities in the empire were Alexandria (Egypt) and Carthage (in what is now Tunisia), each with a population of some 500,000. The Syrian cities of Antioch (now in Turkey) and Apamea had around 200,000 residents each. Ostia, twenty miles downriver from Rome, went from a modest coastal town to a city of 30,000 in the early second century, thanks to the ongoing development of Rome's port facilities there. Pompeii, in southern Italy, had a population of close to 20,000 before it was destroyed by a volcanic eruption in 79 C.E. Most Roman cities, however, especially in the provinces, were home to between 5,000 and 15,000 people. The market town of Virgil's shepherd may have had no more than a few thousand inhabitants.

course military, conquering new territory for Rome. Then, if a new province already had well-established cities, the Roman government used them as headquarters to administer the province. If there were no urban settlements in desirable locations, the Romans built their own. Every legion included the surveyors, architects, carpenters, and stonemasons—along with the manpower provided by the ordinary soldiers—needed for any construction project.

One example of an army-built city is Timgad, in what is now northern Algeria. The emperor Trajan ordered its construction, in 100 C.E., as a settlement for army veterans. These retired soldiers remained on reserve duty, and their town had a strategic location: its nearness to mountain passes allowed it to protect Roman-ruled territory from nomadic groups who lived to the south. The army

Some of the ruins of the North African city of Timgad, including a monumental arch constructed to honor the emperor Trajan

planned and constructed Timgad carefully, with streets laid out in an orderly grid pattern. The city boasted all the comforts of Rome, including fourteen bathhouses.

Even without planning, the Roman legions were responsible for founding numerous cities, many of which still exist today. When the army set up an encampment or built a fort, people from all over the region were attracted to the area. The soldiers, who needed supplies, made excellent customers for local goods and produce. Taverns and other businesses were established to serve the army bases. Many legionnaires formed relationships with local women and had children with them; after the men were discharged from the army, they frequently settled with their families near the camp or fort. As the population grew, a city developed, and as such cities spread through a province, Roman culture—and control—were assured.

II
PUBLIC PLACES AND PRIVATE SPACES

THE ROMAN PEOPLE EASILY FIND EXCELLENT PLACES
IN WHICH TO LIVE.
—VITRUVIUS, *THE TEN BOOKS ON ARCHITECTURE*

magine you are going to visit a Roman city in Italy. The well-paved road you are traveling on leads you through fields and pastures, vineyards and olive groves. As you draw near to the city limits, the road is lined with impressive marble tombs belonging to the families of prominent citizens. The city itself may be walled, and you will have to enter it through an imposing gateway. Except in frontier provinces, city walls and fortified gates are now just symbolic of the empire's might, or they may have been left standing from more turbulent times. But these days, thanks to the *pax Romana,* there is no real need for a city to have such protections. Stay on the road, and it will take you right into the center of the city.

THE HUB OF ACTIVITY

From early times the heart of Rome had been its Forum. In the middle of the Forum was a large rectangular plaza where citizens could gather for political meetings, business discussions, celebrations, ceremonies, and socializing. Around this open area were important temples, the Senate House and other government buildings, and the basilica, a spacious meeting hall where courts of law were held. There were also buildings that housed shops, offices, and schoolrooms. From a platform called the Rostra, emperors and senators made speeches to the people; when a notable person died, a relative might deliver a funeral eulogy from the Rostra. Inscriptions and painted notices on the walls of Forum buildings informed

The forum of a Roman city was a mixture of temples, government buildings, monuments, statues, and open spaces.

citizens of new laws, court decisions, and other important news. The Forum was also the ideal place to erect statues and monuments to honor the emperors and other famous Romans of both past and present.

As Rome grew, the original Forum became too small and crowded to serve the city's population. By 117, five additional forums had been constructed nearby. The last, largest, and most splendid forum of all was built by the emperor Trajan, who paid for the whole thing from the riches of a recent conquest. The buildings in Trajan's forum included two libraries (one for books in Latin, the other for books in Greek) and a grand basilica paved with marble floors and roofed with tiles of gilded bronze. Beside the forum, Trajan had a marketplace constructed. An ancient version of a shopping mall, it housed around 150 shops, supplying the citizens of Rome with both luxuries and everyday needs.

Other cities in the empire had forums of their own. When the Romans took over a city or built a new city in conquered territory, constructing a forum was usually a priority. Forums were often expanded or renovated by emperors, sometimes as a gift when they were visiting a city. Prominent citizens also donated buildings and monuments to their city's forum. For example, one of the largest buildings in Pompeii's forum was a headquarters for the local wool-processing industry, given to the city and the woolworkers by a wealthy widow named Eumachia.

PLACES TO GO, PEOPLE TO MEET

Naturally, the forum was not the only place where a city's residents gathered. Just northeast of Rome's forums was the Campus Martius. This was described during the reign of Augustus by the Greek

geographer Strabo as "an admirably large field on which an enormous number of chariots and horses can race unimpeded and a host of people can daily play ball games and practise discus-throwing and wrestling." The Campus was also the site of temples, tombs, and other monumental structures, as well as of occasional military drills. Many other Roman cities had similar athletic fields.

Nearly every urban neighborhood had a public well or fountain, near which people often lingered for a chat. Marketplaces were good locations for socializing as well as shopping. As in a modern city, friends or business associates frequently met up on the sidewalk; in some Roman cities the sidewalks were shaded by roofs supported by columns. There were taverns, food stands, and cookshops, too.

A nineteenth-century artist imagined this Roman street scene, complete with musicians and a performing monkey to entertain passersby.

A ROMAN BATH

Bathing was an important part of a Roman's daily routine. Women usually bathed in the morning, while men bathed in the afternoon, before dinner. The very wealthy had bathing facilities in their homes, but most city dwellers went to a public bathhouse. The baths were open to everyone who could pay the small entrance fee, and sometimes admission was free, paid for by the emperor or some other dignitary.

A full Roman bath was an elaborate affair. Bathers undressed in a changing room that contained compartments for storing clothes. Then they went into a *sudatorium,* which was like a sauna or steambath. After working up a sweat, they entered a room called the *caldarium.* Here they sprinkled themselves with hot water from a large tub and used a metal scraper to remove dirt and perspiration. (These hot rooms were heated by an underfloor furnace system called a hypocaust.) Next came the *tepidarium,* a warm room where bathers could begin to cool off. Then it was time to move on to the *frigidarium* for a plunge into a cold pool. The last stop was the *unctorium,* where they could be massaged and rubbed with oil.

Large bathhouses had facilities for exercising and socializing as well as for washing. Many had gymnasiums, exercise grounds, ball courts, and swimming pools. There might also be sculpture galleries, gardens, libraries, reading rooms, and rooms for gaming and conversation. Vendors and snack bars sold food and drink to bathers. For the Romans, a bath was as much a form of recreation as a way to get clean.

Though it is now in ruins, this twelve-seater restroom was once part of a public bathhouse in a North African city.

Public bathhouses were among the favorite places for people to meet, whether to socialize or talk business. At one point there were more than eight hundred bathhouses in Rome alone. Many of them were huge, splendid buildings, decorated with colored marble and works of art. Public lavatories (which charged an entrance fee) were also favorite gathering places, for the Romans were experts at making a virtue of a necessity. A public restroom in an ancient Roman city usually had about twenty seats arranged in a semicircle or open rectangle. The seats were often of marble, and behind them niches held statues of heroes, gods, and goddesses. Channels of constantly running water flowed under the seats to carry away sewage. In the middle of the bathroom there might be a fountain, and sometimes the room was heated by a furnace under the floor. For urban Romans, it seemed perfectly natural to sit down to a friendly conversation in these surroundings.

ISLANDS FOR THE MASSES

The majority of Roman city dwellers probably spent as little time as possible in their homes, which tended to be small, dark, cold in the winter, and hot in the summer. There was rarely indoor plumbing—the great water supply brought in by the aqueducts was mainly for public use in fountains, bathhouses, and lavatories. Artificial light was typically supplied by pottery lamps that burned olive oil, although candles might be used in provinces that didn't grow olives. The fireplace had not been invented yet; the usual heat source was a brazier, a kind of pan full of smoldering charcoal, supported by a tripod or other stand. Cooking was generally limited to whatever could be warmed by the brazier.

Such were the conditions in Roman apartment houses, which were called *insulae,* literally "islands." Like islands, these buildings rose up out of the urban "sea," three to five stories tall. A typical *insula* might house between thirty and fifty people. Some buildings had spacious apartments, with windows of mica, clear gypsum, or glass. There might be a central courtyard with a cistern, or tank, to hold water for the tenants' use. The remains of buildings like these are still standing in Ostia, and they are solidly constructed of concrete faced with brick. But a great many *insulae* were slums, shabbily constructed, with cramped apartments and nothing to cover the window openings except wooden shutters or oiled paper. The poet Juvenal wrote of such apartment buildings in Rome: "We inhabit a city propped up for the most part by slats: for that is how the landlord patches up the crack in the old wall, bidding the inmates sleep at ease under the ruin that hangs above their heads."

In more "upscale" *insulae,* the ground floor was often like a private house, occupied by the building's owner or rented by a single family. More commonly, the ground floor of an *insula* was devoted to stores or workshops, which were sometimes little more than booths opening to the street. In either case, this was the only floor that might have a lavatory; people in the upper stories had to make

do with chamber pots, which they were supposed to empty into a vat under the stairs. Sometimes, however, people just dumped the contents of their chamber pots out the window; if they hit a passerby, however, they could be hauled into court and fined.

A model of a street in the port city of Ostia. On the right is a well-built *insula*; at left, a grand single-family home.

A HOUSE IN TOWN

There were more than 46,000 *insulae* in the city of Rome, but only about 1,800 single-family houses—homes of the wealthy and privileged. Even in some of these, rooms on either side of the entryway were used as shops, often run or rented by slaves or freedmen of the family. (The shops were usually walled off from the rest of the building.) Otherwise the only opening on the front of the house was the door—for security and privacy, there were no windows looking out on the street.

The town houses of the wealthy, at least in Italy, generally followed a similar design. The entrance hall led into a large room called an atrium, which was used as a living room and a place to receive guests. Part of the atrium was unroofed, and beneath this opening was a rectangular pool to catch rainwater. Bedrooms and

A HOUSE FOR EVERY LIFESTYLE

One of the treasures of Roman literature is *The Ten Books on Architecture* by Vitruvius, probably written sometime during the reign of Rome's first emperor, Augustus (died 14 C.E.). Vitruvius dedicated this work to the emperor,

> because I saw that you have built and are now building extensively, and that in future also you will take care that our public and private buildings shall be worthy to go down to posterity by the side of your other splendid achievements. I have drawn up definite rules to enable you, by observing them, to have personal knowledge of the quality both of existing buildings and those which are yet to be constructed. For in the following books I have disclosed all the principles of the art [of architecture].

Vitruvius set out to write a complete description of his chosen art, covering such topics as the education of an architect, the properties of different kinds of timber and stone for building, the best place to establish a city and its public buildings, and the proper proportions and designs for temples to various gods and goddesses. The sixth book deals

with private houses. In the following excerpt, Vitruvius describes how houses should be planned "to suit different classes of persons":

Men of everyday fortune do not need entrance courts, tablina, or atriums built in grand style, because such men are more apt to discharge their social obligations by going round to others than to have others come to them.

Those who do business in country produce must have stalls and shops in their entrance courts, with crypts, granaries, storerooms, and so forth in their houses, constructed more for the purpose of keeping the produce in good condition than for ornamental beauty.

For capitalists and farmers of the revenue [businessmen who bid on government contracts, including tax collectors], somewhat comfortable and showy apartments must be constructed, secure against robbery; for advocates [lawyers] and public speakers, handsomer and more roomy, to accommodate meetings; for men of rank who, from holding offices and magistracies, have social obligations to their fellow-citizens, lofty entrance courts in regal style, and most spacious atriums and peristyles, with plantations [gardens] and walks of some extent in them, appropriate to their dignity. They need also libraries, picture galleries, and basilicas, finished in a style similar to that of great public buildings, since public councils as well as private law suits and hearings before arbitrators are very often held in the houses of such men.

A Roman bedroom decorated with beautifully frescoed walls. The mosaic floor combines geometric designs with a scene from mythology.

sitting rooms opened off the atrium. Toward the back, on either side, were recesses that housed small statues or paintings of the family's ancestors and protector gods. Behind the atrium was the *tablinum,* where the head of the family had his office. Next to the *tablinum* was a common location for the dining room. At the back of the house there was usually a peristyle, a courtyard or garden area surrounded by a covered walkway. Rooms opening off the peristyle might include the kitchen, slave quarters, storerooms, and sometimes a bath, a lavatory, and a stable. Really large and luxurious houses had even more rooms. For example, one lavish house in Pompeii had two atriums and two peristyles. There could also be an additional dining room, an extra room for entertaining, a picture gallery, a library, and elaborate gardens.

A family's wealth and culture were expressed by the way the

house was decorated, with mosaic floors, frescoed walls, and elegant fountains and sculptures in the peristyle or garden. Mosaics were often done in abstract designs or geometric patterns, but sometimes they made elaborate pictures or spelled out messages (such as *Cave canem,* "Beware of the dog," found in

A wordless "Beware of the dog" mosaic from the entryway to a Roman home

many entryways). Frescoes could also be abstract, but often they showed landscapes or scenes from mythology. Dining rooms frequently had frescoes or mosaics depicting fruit, shellfish, or other types of food. This was an example of the Roman devotion to propriety, one of the most important elements of architecture according to the architect Vitruvius, who called propriety "that perfection of style which comes when a work is authoritatively constructed on approved principles."

WORKING FOR A LIVING

HELLO PROFIT!
—MOSAIC FLOOR FROM POMPEII

With no really effective artificial light sources, the Romans depended almost completely on natural light. To take the best advantage of daylight, they were usually up by sunrise. Breakfast was a quick meal of bread and perhaps cheese, washed down with water. Then it was off to work. Many shopkeepers and craftsmen lived in lofts above their stores or workshops, or in rooms behind them. Other workers would have to head through the crowded streets to their jobs.

Main streets in Roman cities were generally paved with stone and had raised sidewalks on either side. There were pedestrian crossings with stepping stones that led from sidewalk to sidewalk. The stepping stones helped protect people from mud and animal

opposite:
A food vendor sells round loaves of bread from his stall in a public square in Pompeii.

Stepping stones like these, in Pompeii, helped people get from one sidewalk to another with relatively clean, dry feet.

droppings in the street. Most people traveled about the city on foot. The wealthy, however, might ride in litters or chairs carried by slaves. Wheeled traffic was banned between sunrise and dusk, with the exception of dignitaries' chariots on specific special occasions and wagons hauling materials for building projects. So those who made their living by carting goods into the city were forced to do their work in the dark of night.

SLAVE LABOR

Slavery was a fact of life in the Roman Empire, as it was throughout the ancient world. It was very common to take huge numbers of captives from a country defeated in war, and for some time Rome's conquests supplied the empire with most of its slaves. After the empire's borders became more settled, the majority of slaves were people born into slavery, for the children of slaves were also slaves.

Historians estimate that slaves made up about 30 percent of Rome's population. The city itself owned a number of slaves, who did administrative work, maintained the aqueducts, cleaned and repaired streets and public buildings, and worked on construction projects. Some wealthy Romans owned hundreds of slaves, and even people with modest incomes might have one or two. Some slaves worked in or even ran businesses for their masters; others were rented out to people who only needed a slave for a short time. Still other slaves were entertainers of one kind or another: gladiators, chariot racers, actors, singers, dancers, and acrobats. A large number of urban slaves worked in their owners' households as secretaries, accountants, librarians, doctors, midwives, wet nurses, teachers, hairdressers, barbers, maids, masseurs, cooks, launderers, housecleaners, doorkeepers, litter carriers, torchbearers, and so on.

Barbarians defeated in war, like the man on the ground here, often became slaves consigned to do heavy manual labor.

The Roman economy was greatly dependent on slave labor. Keeping slaves from rebelling, therefore, was always a concern. Until the second half of the first century, slaves had no legal standing or protection, and owners could treat them however they wanted. Some masters used violence or the fear of violence to keep slaves obedient. We read of a cook being beaten for burning a meal, of a lady's maid having her hair pulled and her clothing torn for not curling her mistress's hair properly.

In 61 C.E. a mistreated slave killed his master, a high-ranking city official in Rome. The victim's friends wanted all four hundred of his slaves put to death, to discourage other slaves who might think of murdering their owners. Many Romans protested against this cruel punishment. The Senate debated the matter and finally decided to allow the mass execution. As one senator put it, "You cannot control these dregs of society except through fear."

Other Romans, however, felt that it was better to treat slaves with some kindness and respect. Well-treated slaves who had the hope of eventually gaining their freedom were more likely to accept their state of servitude. Besides, some Romans argued, to treat slaves decently was simply the right and humane thing to do. This idea was expressed by the playwright-philosopher-statesman Seneca the Younger when he wrote to a friend,

> I was happy to learn from people who had just visited you that you live on friendly terms with your slaves. . . . Some people say, "They're just slaves." But they are our fellow human beings! "They're just slaves." But they live with us! "They're just slaves." In fact, they are our fellow slaves, if you stop to consider that fate has as much control over us as it has over them. . . . I don't want to engage in a lengthy discussion of the treatment of slaves, toward whom we are very arrogant, very cruel, and very abusive. However, this is the essence of my advice: "Treat those of lower social rank as you would wish to be treated by those of higher social rank."

Household slaves were generally more fortunate than other slaves. Many were given an education or training in skilled crafts. Slaves who worked closely with their owners often had the opportunity to get to know them well, and a kind of friendship could grow between master and slave. Such slaves might receive gifts of money from their masters and even from their masters' friends; slaves were frequently able to save up enough to buy their freedom.

Pressing grapes into wine was only one of the tasks assigned to slaves who worked on country estates.

Owners sometimes freed slaves out of gratitude for their service; it was very common for people to write a will that freed many or all of their slaves. There were even cases of childless couples freeing then adopting a favorite slave.

Freedmen and freedwomen often continued doing the same jobs they had performed as slaves. They still had to show loyalty and work a certain number of days a year for their former owners. But freed slaves became Roman citizens, with voting rights for the men. The children of freedpersons were completely free and, if they were wealthy enough, could even run for public office and rise to the top ranks of Roman society. However, few attained this level of success.

GOODS AND SERVICES

In a Roman city, a large number of jobs could be done by slaves, freedpersons, or freeborn people of the lower class. Regardless of their status as free or slave, workers in the same craft or trade

Cushion makers in Rome show their wares to prospective customers.

banded together in some cities to form what we might call guilds. These associations hosted dinners for their members and often paid members' funeral expenses. Like modern trade unions, the guilds also endorsed political candidates. Graffiti from walls in the southern Italian city of Pompeii campaigned to passersby with slogans such as, "The muleteers urge the election of Gaius Julius Polybius."

The goods produced in Roman cities might be used locally or shipped to other parts of the empire. Many Romans were skilled artisans, among them leatherworkers, woodworkers, stoneworkers, and metalworkers. Some produced luxury items such as dyes, cosmetics, perfumes, jewelry, mosaics, furniture, wall paintings, and garden ornaments. Numerous shops were small individual or family businesses, where the artisan both made and sold goods in the same place. There were also large workshops or factories employing many people, which produced a variety of foodstuffs and manufactured goods, for example fish sauce, olive oil, wine, pottery, lamps, bricks, glassware, and cloth. Providing food and drink kept numerous city workers busy, including bakers, butchers, fishmongers, chicken sellers, innkeepers, and snack-bar operators. Then there were auctioneers, town criers, carters, porters, water carriers, boatmen, bathhouse attendants, sewer cleaners, construction

A baker tends his oven.

workers, veterinarians—the list of occupations could go on and on. In addition, in many urban areas some people went out every day to work on farms outside the city limits.

Even with so many jobs to do, however, there were people who couldn't get work, especially in Rome. Some worked as day laborers or did odd jobs. Even some workers with full-time employment could not earn enough to support their families. Urban rents were very high, and so were other prices. For example, a pound of chicken could cost a tailor a full day's wages; a pair of boots for a mule driver cost him nearly five days' earnings. Freeborn workers had no healthcare plans, unemployment insurance, or other job benefits. For all of these reasons, free Romans sometimes had a much harder time than many slaves whose masters provided them with food, clothing, housing, and medical care.

PREJUDICE AGAINST FOREIGNERS
AND FREEDMEN

Many of Rome's workers were freedpersons or immigrants from Greek-speaking cities in the East. Some Romans resented these people contributing "foreign ideas" to society and "taking jobs away" from free citizens. The satirists Martial and Juvenal both expressed this prejudice, sometimes in an exaggerated manner. "Grammarian, orator, geometer, painter, wrestling-master, prophet, tightrope walker, medical man, wizard—he can do anything, your penniless Greek," Juvenal commented sarcastically. Martial complained:

> Fortune, do you really think this situation is fair? Maevius, who was not born in Syria or Parthia or bought at a Cappadocian slave auction, but who was native-born, . . . a citizen who is pleasant, honest, a blameless friend, who knows both Latin and Greek . . . shivers in a cheap gray garment, while Incitatus, a freedman, a former mule driver, shines forth in scarlet.

The satiric novelist Petronius made one of his characters, a freedman, answer these kinds of objections with the following indignant speech to a dinner guest who had been making fun of him.

> I hope that I now conduct my life so that no one can laugh at me. I'm a man among men; I hold up my head when I walk; I don't owe anyone a cent. . . . I bought

myself a bit of land and saved up some cash. I feed twenty bellies and a dog.* I bought freedom for the slave woman who had shared my bed.** . . . For my own freedom I paid 1000 silver coins. . . . I was a slave for forty years. . . . I arrived in this town when I was a young boy. . . . I worked hard, and pleased my master. . . . I made my way success-fully—and that's real success! Being born a free man is as easy as saying "Boo." So what are you staring at now, you stupid, smelly goat?

*In other words, he is now well off enough to maintain his own household, including a number of slaves.
**Slave marriages were not legal, but slave couples still formed lasting relationships.

~IV~
ROMAN MEN:
FROM HIGH TO LOW

IF YOU ASK SOMEONE, "WHAT DID YOU DO TODAY?" HE WILL
ANSWER, "I WENT TO A COMING-OF-AGE PARTY; I ATTENDED AN
ENGAGEMENT PARTY AND THEN A WEDDING; ONE MAN ASKED ME TO
BE A WITNESS AT THE SIGNING OF HIS WILL, ANOTHER ASKED ME FOR
LEGAL ADVICE, A THIRD ASKED ME TO SIT IN COURT."
—PLINY THE YOUNGER, *LETTERS*

Father knows best" could have been ancient
Rome's motto. The Romans called their country
patria, "the fatherland." This is the root of our word *patri-
otic*, and comes from the Latin word for "father," *pater*.
For the Romans, father and country were inseparable.
Their whole society revolved around their ideas of the duties and
privileges of fathers. The *pater familias*, "father of a family," was the
head of the household, with absolute authority over every member
of his family. He was responsible for their support and welfare, and
also exercised whatever discipline was necessary to make sure that
they behaved as proper members of society. It was his right to decide
even who they married (or divorced) and what they did for a living.
The Roman state worked in a similar way. The upper class, who

opposite:
A group of
senators, men
at the highest
level of Roman
society

controlled virtually everything, were called *patricii* (patricians), "those with fatherly qualities."* One of the highest honors a Roman man could receive was to be named *pater patriae*, "father of the fatherland," and Roman emperors were often given this title. The state was thought of as a very large extended family, which the emperor was supposed to oversee like a stern but caring father.

PATRONS AND CLIENTS

Another word related to *pater* was *patronus,* "defender." In ancient Rome a *patronus,* or patron, was a man whom a number of other men depended on to look out for their interests, advise them, help them in times of trouble, give them gifts, and so on. These were the patron's clients. They in turn owed the patron loyalty and various services, such as accompanying him to the forum when he had important business there or campaigning and voting for him in local elections. The more clients a man had, the more influence he had, and the higher his status was. One of the reasons that the emperor Augustus was able to rise to power was that he had a huge number of clients, probably more than any other man in Rome.

Freed slaves became their former masters' clients. Freeborn men also had patrons, and even a patron with a number of clients would have a patron of his own, a man of higher rank. Patronage was a kind of ladder, where every man was a client of someone on the rung above him. At the top of the ladder was the emperor. He alone had no patron, except perhaps Jupiter, the chief god of the Roman state.

Almost the first thing a Roman man did after getting up was go to wish his patron good morning. This visit was a show of respect, and the patron might have some errand or task he wanted a client

*More information about Rome's upper class, including the emperors and their families, can be found in another book in this series, *The Patricians*.

GREEDY CLIENTS AND RUDE PATRONS

The patron-client relationship had been an important part of Roman life for hundreds of years. By the middle of the first century, however, many a client seemed to have little real respect for his patron. As Seneca the Younger expressed the situation in one of his letters, "Once upon a time, clients sought a politically powerful friend; now they seek loot." The poet Martial wrote about what happened when he forgot to use the title *dominus*, "lord," when speaking to his patron: "This morning I address[ed] you, as it chanced, by your own name, nor did I add 'My Lord' . . . Do you ask how much such casual conduct has cost me? It has robbed me of a hundred farthings." That was the risk a client took for offending his patron—the client might not receive his usual handout, money that he sometimes depended on to buy food or pay his rent.

Patrons could also behave disrespectfully. In one of his essays, Seneca the Younger complained about haughty patrons who acted as though it was an annoying chore to receive their clients' morning greetings:

How many patrons are there who drive away their clients by staying in bed when they call, or ignoring their presence, or being rude? How many are there who rush off on a pretense of urgent business after keeping the poor client waiting for a long time? How many avoid going through an atrium packed with clients and escape through a secret back door, as if it were not ruder to avoid a client than to turn him away? How many . . . will yawn disdainfully at men who have interrupted their own sleep in order to wait upon his [the patron's] awakening, and will mumble a greeting through half-open lips, and will need to be reminded a thousand times of the client's name?

to do. The client generally hoped to receive a gift or handout, or perhaps a dinner invitation. Most patrons invited their clients to dinner now and then, and often this was the only time a poor man had a really good meal. A stingy or arrogant patron, however, might serve his clients inferior food and drink, while higher-ranking guests at the same dinner joined the host in a meal of the best quality.

UPPER-CLASS TASKS

Men with the rank of senator were at the top of Roman society. They did not have to work for a living; in fact, it was actually illegal for them to earn money through their own labor. Senators were the great landowners of the empire, and most of their income came from the sale of the produce on their farming estates. With agents acting for them, members of the senatorial class also profited from property rentals, business investments, and moneylending.

Because senators were the wealthiest of Roman citizens, they were expected to devote themselves to government service. And only the rich *could* afford to serve in the government: not only were officeholders unpaid, but they were expected to spend a great deal of their own money on public works, entertainments, and gifts to the common people. Even when they served as lawyers, they worked for free.

One of the most important senators in Rome was the city prefect, who was appointed by the emperor. Responsible for maintaining law and order, he commanded the urban cohort, as many as 4,500 soldiers who formed a kind of police force. The city prefect also inspected markets to make sure meat prices were fair, and he had the power to prohibit individuals from engaging in business, professional, or legal activities.

⊷ DRESSING FOR SUCCESS ↝

Nothing says "Roman" like the toga, the garment that clothed male citizens for centuries. The toga was an oblong of heavy white woolen cloth, roughly eighteen feet in length. It was worn over a tunic of linen or wool that reached to the knees. A man wrapped the toga around himself (usually with some assistance) in complicated drapes and folds. One part of the cloth hung from the left shoulder to the right thigh in a way that formed a pocket. Another part of the toga draped so that it could be pulled up over the head as a hood, which was necessary for religious ceremonies.

The toga was difficult to put on and often cumbersome to wear. Another problem was that it was supposed to be kept sparkling white, which meant that it frequently had to be sent to the cleaner's for a good scrubbing. This made it wear out rather quickly—fortunately, patrons traditionally gave each client a new toga every year. This was a good thing, since clients were expected to wear the toga when making the morning visit to their patrons.

Many men took off their togas whenever they could, preferring the simple comfort of their tunics. A light, full-skirted kind of tunic called a *synthesis* became the preferred wear for dinner parties. (Fashion-conscious men might change into a different *synthesis* for each course of the meal.) Eventually, so many men were running around without their togas that several emperors passed laws to make sure that Rome's male citizens dressed with proper dignity. During the second century the emperor Hadrian, for example, ordered senators and equestrians "to wear the toga whenever they appeared in public except when they were returning from a banquet."

Below the senators ranked the equestrians. To belong to this class, a man did not have to be as wealthy as a senator, but he was still far richer than the majority of people in the empire. Equestrians were typically involved in "big business," making money as importers and exporters, shipowners, bankers, bidders on government contracts, and the like. Some military and government positions were open to equestrians, and these opportunities increased as the empire went on.

While Rome's government was in the hands of the emperor and his appointees, in many other cities of the empire men of the upper classes could run for election to town offices. The graffiti from Pompeii show that local political life could be quite lively. Elections were held every year to choose two *duovirs,* or co-mayors, and an aedile, who supervised the markets, public buildings, and public works. Often there was also some kind of town council, made up of wealthy freeborn men.

ARMY LIFE

Soldiers were a familiar sight in Roman cities—but not always a welcome sight. In camp soldiers lived according to strict discipline, but when they were out on the town they had a reputation for bullying civilians. Since a soldier could only be disciplined by his commander, a civilian filing a complaint had little hope of justice, as Juvenal pointed out in one of his *Satires:* "Your teeth are shattered? Face hectically inflamed, with great black welts? You know the doctor wasn't too optimistic about the eye that was left. But it's not a bit of good your running to the courts about it. If you've been beaten up by a soldier, better keep it to yourself."

For some 125,000 to 165,000 men, the army was their career for

most of their lives. The requirements for joining the Roman legions were strict. Recruits had to be Roman citizens*, and they had to meet high standards of physical fitness. They had to be mentally tough, too, with a strong team spirit, and for good reason: When the army was on campaign, the soldiers lived in leather tents, eight men to a tent. On the march, each group of eight shared a mule, which carried the tent and some supplies. The men themselves carried not only their weapons but also the necessary equipment for any construction projects they might have to undertake. The first-century historian Josephus described a Roman legion on the march this way:

Then they march forward, everyone silent and in correct order, each man maintaining his particular position in the

Roman soldiers, including (far right) a *cornicen*, or military horn player. The Roman army used horns and trumpets to signal various commands to the troops.

*All freeborn Italians were citizens. Freeborn people in the provinces became citizens as a reward for service to the empire. Freed slaves, whether in Italy or the provinces, automatically received citizenship along with their freedom. The children of citizens also held Roman citizenship. Only citizens enjoyed the full protection of the law.

ranks, just as he would in battle. The infantry are equipped with breastplates and helmets, and carry a sword on both sides. . . . The infantry chosen to guard the general carry a spear and a small round shield. The rest of the soldiers carry a javelin and an oblong shield. However, they also carry a saw, a basket, a shovel, and an ax, as well as a leather strap, a scythe, a chain, and three days' food rations. As a result, an infantryman differs little from a loaded pack mule.

Serving in the Roman legions was far more of a commitment than enlisting in a modern army. Once a man joined up, he was required to stay for twenty-five years. If he deserted and was caught, he was executed. Discipline was harsh, and training was rigorous.

Roman foot soldiers, armed with spears and shields, accompanied by mounted troops who functioned mainly as scouts and messengers

The cost of a soldier's armor, equipment, and food was deducted from his pay. Legions were generally stationed near the empire's frontiers, or in trouble spots far from Italy. Moreover, until 197 C.E. legionary soldiers were not allowed to marry (although they frequently had long-term, but unofficial, relationships with women who lived near the army bases).

The army offered some opportunities for promotion. An ambitious man might rise to the rank of centurion, a commander who earned as much as sixty times the pay of ordinary legionnaires. Retired centurions often became important, respected men in their communities. Every soldier who survived his twenty-five years of service received a retirement bonus that equalled close to fourteen years' pay. The hope of such rewards was enough to make the army an appealing career choice for many men, especially those who had few other opportunities. The historian Tacitus, a senator during the first century, remarked on this fact a little scornfully: "It is chiefly the needy and the homeless who adopt by their own choice a soldier's life."

V

CITY WOMEN

GUARDIANS ARE APPOINTED . . . FOR FEMALES BOTH BEFORE AND
AFTER PUBERTY BECAUSE THEY ARE THE WEAKER SEX AND ARE
IGNORANT IN BUSINESS AND LEGAL MATTERS. . . .
—ULPIAN, *RULES*

In many ways, the Roman Empire was a man's world. Women had far fewer rights and opportunities than they have in most industrialized nations today. Even women who were full Roman citizens could not vote or hold office. Women had to have male guardians to handle their legal and financial affairs.* However, women could inherit money and property and often were able to control it themselves thanks to loopholes in the law. We know that many wealthy city women used some of their money to benefit their communities by funding building projects and charities. Unfortunately, we do not know as much about ancient Roman women as we would like to, since nearly all the surviving writings are from men's points of view—and few male authors were interested in writing about women's lives.

opposite:
**This richly
colored fresco
portrays a
woman of
Pompeii.**

*Freeborn women could be released from guardianship after having three children; freedwomen earned the same privilege after bearing four children. Guardianship rules gradually loosened: by the middle of the second century, a woman could make out her own will without her guardian's advice or approval.

A well-to-do young woman who enjoys the finer things: her hair is fashionably dyed blond, her bracelets are gold, and she is refilling a flask of perfume.

WEALTHY WIVES

The amount—and kind—of freedom a woman enjoyed depended largely on her wealth and social class. An upper-class woman had many slaves to help her in the home, so she was able to go out to visit friends, exercise and relax at the baths, or attend public shows. She could also spend her leisure time reading, playing board games, or playing a musical instrument. A few upper-class women wrote poetry or other works, though little of these survive. Many Roman men, however, were offended if women showed too much intelligence, as Juvenal expressed in his *Satires:* "Don't marry a woman who speaks like an orator—or knows every history book. There should be some things in books which she doesn't understand. I hate a woman who . . . always obeys all the laws and rules of correct speech, who quotes verses I've never even heard of."

The ideal for Roman women, especially of the upper classes, was often portrayed in funeral eulogies such as this one for a woman named Murdia: "My dearest mother won the greatest praise of all, because she was like other good women in her modesty, decency, chastity, obedience, wool-work, zeal and loyalty. . . ." These were the qualities that Roman men valued most in wives, mothers, and daughters. Woolworking, by the way, was traditionally women's main work: spinning thread, weaving cloth, and sewing the family's clothes. In the early empire, many upper-class women still did these things themselves; later, they usually only oversaw the woolworking of their household slaves.

An upper-class Roman woman's main duty was to bear and raise children. This was, in fact, a dangerous job. Even with the best doctor or midwife, there was a lot that could go wrong during pregnancy and childbirth, and a large number of mothers and babies died. Miscarriages were also common. Many women had trouble getting pregnant in the first place. For all of these reasons, most upper-class women had only one to three children, even though large families were the ideal.

WORKING CLASS WOMEN

While women of the upper classes enjoyed freedom from hard work, they had little control over their personal lives. Their marriages were always arranged, frequently for the sake of financial or political advantages for their fathers. For the same reasons, fathers could (and did) order daughters to divorce and then marry men with better connections. Divorce was not unusual in ancient Rome, and the children remained with their father.

In contrast, lower-class women might choose their own husbands. We have many examples of tombstones belonging to couples who met while they were slaves. Slaves were not allowed to marry, but people formed lasting relationships anyway. A slave who was freed often bought the freedom of his or her partner so that the two could be legally married. Freed slaves and freeborn workers alike might meet future spouses among their coworkers in shops or factories. Among poorer Romans, there was more opportunity for marriage to be based on love and friendship, since political and financial influences were not an issue.

Poorer Romans, however, had to work hard to earn a living. Many women worked only in the home, spinning, weaving, sewing, cooking, cleaning, and raising their children. Sometimes they sold some of the thread they spun or pieces of cloth they wove. Other women might assist their husbands in home-based family busi-

This wife and husband appear to have a close and caring relationship.

nesses. Still others held jobs outside the home or had their own businesses. This may have been especially true of freedwomen, who had often learned and practiced various trades while slaves.

The evidence for Roman working women often makes it difficult to tell if they were slaves, freedwomen, or freeborn women; probably women of all three groups frequently worked side by side, and oftentimes labored alongside men, too. Historians have learned that women worked at a variety of crafts and trades; among others, we know of women who were weavers, menders, dye makers, doctors, midwives, wet nurses, maids, secretaries, hairdressers, dressmakers, perfumers, actresses, dancers, innkeepers, waitresses, bathhouse attendants, shopkeepers, fruit and vegetable sellers, fishmongers, moneylenders, and property owners.

A Roman woman's shop, where she sells poultry, pork, and rabbit

CITY WOMEN

Portrait of a woman from Herculaneum

LITERARY WOMEN

For the most part, literary activities (besides reading) were for men. We do know of a small number of women, though, who were writers. One of these was Sulpicia, who lived in Rome toward the end of the first century B.C.E. Only fragments of a few of Sulpicia's poems survive. Here is a portion of one written in the voice of a young woman, addressed to her guardian, in which she worries about leaving Rome for the countryside, where she will have to spend her birthday apart from her beloved, Cerinthus:

> My hateful birthday is at hand, which I must celebrate
>   without Cerinthus in the irksome countryside.
> What can be sweeter than the City? Or is a country villa
>   fit for a girl, or the chilly river in the fields of Arezzo?
> Take a rest, Messalla, don't pay so much attention to me;
>   journeys, my dear relative, are often untimely.
> When I'm taken away, I leave my mind and feelings here,
>   since force keeps me from acting as my own master.

Another literary woman was Pamphila of Epidaurus, Greece, who lived around the middle of the first century C.E. The daughter of a learned man, she married a scholar and became extremely interested in history. Pamphila wrote thirty-three books of history, which were much read even a hundred years after her death. They are lost now, but a ninth-century author still knew of Pamphila and summarized her introduction to her work:

> She says that after thirteen years of living with her husband since she was a child, she began to put together these historical materials and recorded what she had learned from her husband during those thirteen years . . . and whatever she happened to hear from anyone else visiting him (for there were many visitors with a reputation for learning). And she added to this what she had read in books.

We can assume—or at least hope—that there were other women like Pamphila who enjoyed the satisfactions of learning.

·VI·

AN URBAN CHILDHOOD

PRAISE LIFTS THE SPIRIT AND MAKES A CHILD SELF-CONFIDENT,
BUT TOO MUCH PRAISE MAKES HIM INSOLENT AND BAD-TEMPERED.
—SENECA THE YOUNGER, *AN ESSAY ABOUT ANGER*

All Roman babies were born at home. After birth, the child was laid at its father's feet. If the father picked up the baby, it would be raised by the family. Otherwise the child was exposed—taken outside and left in some public place to die or to be found and raised by someone else. Occasionally an abandoned baby might be taken in by a childless couple who would truly love and care for it. More often, people who picked up these children were slave dealers.

This was one of the harsh facts of life among the Roman poor: parents who already had more children than they could afford to feed sometimes felt they had no choice but to expose their newborn. There were no reliable methods of family planning, no foster-care systems, no adoption agencies. The lack of advanced medical treat-

opposite:
A child grasps a lock of his affectionate father's hair.

51

ments also led people to abandon babies with birth defects. And fathers rejected female infants more often than males, since boys would have a greater ability to contribute to the family income.

Historians cannot be certain how common it was for babies to be abandoned during the first two centuries of the empire. It was an ancient custom, and there were no laws against it. A letter has been found from Roman-ruled Egypt, written in 1 B.C.E. by a husband who had to leave his family to find work. He wrote home to his pregnant wife, "If I receive my pay soon, I will send it up to you. If you have the baby before I return, if it is a boy, let it live; if it is a girl, expose it."

PLAYTIME AND SCHOOL DAYS

Even a baby who wasn't exposed was not sure to survive. Roughly 25 percent of Roman infants died during their first year, and perhaps 25 percent of those who made it to age one died by age ten. So the survival of a healthy child, in a family with the means to care for it, was a source of great joy. Parents generally did all they could to ensure that their children thrived, even taking precautions against supernatural forces. For example, most Roman children wore a *bulla,* a circular pendant made of gold (for the well-off) or leather (for the poor), for protection against evil spirits.

Like children throughout history, Roman children liked toys, games, pets, and sweet treats. Boys and girls in wealthy families, of course, had more opportunities to enjoy these things. Some of the toys available were dolls (made of rags, wood, or bone), model chariots, tops, marbles, hobbyhorses, and wooden swords. There were board games resembling backgammon and checkers. Another game, knucklebones, usually played with the anklebones of goats,

Roman children made toys out of whatever was available. These little boys are playing with nuts.

may have been like jacks. Then there were games similar to hide-and-seek, leapfrog, and blindman's buff. A wide variety of ball games could be enjoyed by children of all ages.

Children's education usually began at home. Parents taught manners, moral principles, and religious beliefs, and probably told stories about their ancestors and great heroes of the past. In prosperous families, trusted slaves also took part in raising and teaching the children. Many wealthy children, particularly boys, were educated at home by private tutors for years. Other boys, and some girls, began attending elementary school around the age of seven.

The school day began as soon as it was light out. Students went home for lunch at midday, but might have more classes afterward. Schools were usually held in shops, small apartments, or public places such as the forum or even on the sidewalk. Students might have chairs, but there were no desks. Sometimes books were used, and the pupils had wooden tablets coated with wax; they used a writing instrument called a stylus to scratch their exercises into the wax. Oftentimes the teacher would simply recite literary passages to the students, who memorized and recited them back. Many teachers beat students who did poorly. Enlightened educators, such as the orator Quintilian, recommended a different approach for teaching a child:

> Let his lessons be fun, let him volunteer answers, let him be praised, and let him learn the pleasure of doing well. If, on occasion, he refuses instruction, bring in someone to serve as a rival, someone with whom he can compete; but let him think that he is doing well more often than not. Encourage him with the rewards or prizes in which his age group delights.

A teacher scolds a late-arriving student while another pupil reads from a scroll.

In elementary school, children learned basic reading, writing, and arithmetic. They also memorized legends, laws, poems, and wise sayings. This was where schooling ended for most Romans—there was no free public education, and most parents could not afford to pay a schoolteacher for more than a few years, if that. Some boys, however, went on to grammar school around the age of ten or eleven. Here they polished their writing ability, studied public speaking and poetry, and learned Greek (if they didn't already know it). They might also study some astronomy, science, music, and philosophy. At the age of fourteen or fifteen, a few boys—usually only those from the upper classes—received advanced training in public speaking and law.

BECOMING AN ADULT

Adult responsibilities came early to most Romans. Slave children and children from very poor families might start working by the age when others were going to elementary school. For example, we have this gravestone inscription for a girl who made women's hairnets: "Viccentia, sweetest daughter, maker of gold nets, who lived for nine years and nine months." Even most boys who went to elementary school probably started working for a living before they were teenagers. If a father practiced a skilled craft or trade, he generally taught it to his sons, who then worked alongside him. Other boys might serve an apprenticeship learning a trade from a neighbor or relative. Many boys had no chance to learn any skills and had to take whatever work they could get.

A boy officially became an adult at around sixteen. The day he came of age was usually one of celebration. First the boy left his *bulla* and his purple-bordered childhood toga at the shrine of his

❧ A GRATEFUL SON ❧

Horace, who lived during the reign of Augustus, was one of Rome's greatest poets and enjoyed the favor of the emperor himself. This was in spite of the fact that his background was very humble. In the following selection, Horace looks back on his school days and pays tribute to his father for placing him on the road to success:

My father deserves all the credit. For although he was a poor man, with only an infertile plot of land, he was not content to send me to Flavius's school [the school in Horace's hometown] which the burly sons of burly centurions attended, carrying their book-bags and writing tablets slung over their left shoulders. . . . My father had the courage to take his boy to Rome, to have him taught the same skills which any equestrian or senator would have his sons taught. If anyone had seen my clothing or the slaves that attended me, as is the custom in a large city, he would have thought that my expenses were being paid for from an ancestral estate. But my paedagogus [chaperone, usually a slave], my absolutely incorruptible guardian, was my father who accompanied me to school. . . . He didn't make these sacrifices because he worried that someone might criticize him if I became a crier [a town crier, who might also work as an auctioneer] or, like him, a money-collector; nor would I have complained if he hadn't taken me to Rome. But as it is now, he deserves from me unstinting gratitude and praise. I could never be ashamed of such a father, nor do I feel any need, as many people do, to apologize for being a freedman's son.

family's protector deities. Then he put on the pure white toga of manhood. After a visit to the forum, his family and friends gave him a party. If he belonged to the upper classes, he was now able to begin his career in government or business. A lower-class boy could now join the army if he wanted to.

There was no coming-of-age ceremony for girls. After elementary school (if they got to attend at all), they began preparing for marriage, learning the skills they would need to run a household. By the time a girl was a teenager, she was usually married or at least engaged, especially if she belonged to the upper classes. (Daughters of wealthy families tended to marry in their early teens, or even younger; women of the lower classes might not marry till their mid to late teens.) Her father or guardian chose her husband, who was generally quite a bit older than she was; he might even be in his forties or fifties and have been married before.

The night before her wedding, the bride gave away her toys to younger friends and relatives and laid her *bulla* in the family shrine. Very early on the wedding morning, her mother dressed her in her bridal garments, which included a yellow-orange veil crowned with a wreath of flowers. The wedding ceremony took place in the bride's home, with the couple joining hands and stating their consent to be married. In the evening, after a banquet, a lively torchlit procession escorted the bride to her new home. After she was carried over the threshold (for good luck), two bridesmaids brought in her distaff and spindle, with which she would spin wool, symbolizing her new life as a married woman.

·VII·

REST AND RECREATION

HUNTING, BATHING, GAMING, LAUGHING—THAT IS LIVING.
—MOSAIC PAVEMENT FROM THE FORUM OF TIMGAD

lthough the workday began early, for a great many free Romans it ended in midafternoon. Then it was time to visit the baths, where some men might spend most of the rest of the day. Others might go for a stroll after bathing, or meet up with friends at a tavern or snack bar. There they would pass the time drinking, gambling, and talking. Respectable women did not go to taverns, but they could attend dinner parties and similar private social functions. On most holidays—and there were well over one hundred a year—there were free public entertainments that anyone could attend.

opposite: An Egyptian entertainer juggles eggs at a Roman party. This painting is by Lawrence Alma-Tadema, a nineteenth-century artist who was famous for his well-researched portrayals of life in the ancient world.

BOUNTIFUL BANQUETS

Dinnertime arrived in late afternoon. Poor people usually ate very simply, sitting on stools in their apartments and perhaps having little more than porridge and beans, unless they were invited to dine at their patron's home. For well-to-do Romans, giving or attending a dinner party was a favorite form of recreation. These dinners might be relatively small and simple, or they could be lavish banquets with exotic foods and elaborate entertainment. In good weather they were often held outside in the garden or peristyle.

A Roman dining room or outdoor dining area typically contained three couches arranged around a low table. Diners reclined, leaning on their left elbows, three to a couch. They ate with spoons, knives, and their fingers. Slaves waited on them and brought them water for hand washing whenever necessary. For some special outdoor dinners, the couches were set around a garden pool, and the guests selected morsels of food from boat-shaped floating dishes.

A Roman dinner generally had three courses, but there could be several dishes in each course. First came appetizers, which were often egg dishes, fish, and raw vegetables. The main course featured meats and cooked vegetables. Choices for dessert included fruit, pastries, and cakes. The usual drink was wine.

The entertainment during and after a meal depended on the host's wealth and tastes. Many diners were satisfied simply with good conversation. Slaves often provided music while guests were eating. Between courses there might be performances by singers, dancers, actors, or acrobats. Upper-class men with literary interests often held recitations as part of the after-dinner entertainment. They would read aloud from their own writings, or from the works of famous authors.

ᴇᴀᴛ LIKE A ROMAN

Here is a simple menu similar to what a reasonably well-off Roman might have eaten for dinner. If you also want to drink like a Roman, you can serve grape juice instead of wine, but it should be at room temperature.

Gustatio (Appetizers)
- Scrambled eggs topped with tuna, finely chopped raw onions, and fresh rosemary.
- Fresh watercress with a dressing made of Worcestershire sauce (1 T.), red-wine or cider vinegar (1 T.), olive oil (3 T.), and black pepper to taste. (The Worcestershire sauce is a substitution for a sauce made from pickled fish that the Romans used in much of their cooking.)

Prima Mensa (Main Course)
- Small sausages served on a bed of couscous or Cream of Wheat. (Romans ate a lot of wheat porridge and similar grain dishes.)
- Steamed carrot strips, reheated with a little olive oil and cumin.
- Cooked white beans with bacon crumbled on top. (Fava beans would be most authentic, but you could use cannellini, or white kidney beans, instead.)

Secunda Mensa (Dessert)
- Roasted chestnuts (these can be bought canned) dipped in honey.
- Fresh pears and apple slices sprinkled with cinnamon and raisins.

Clients were expected to attend recitations by their patron (and to praise him enthusiastically), and many men felt that going to recitations was a boring duty. Others, however, looked forward to these literary dinners, as Pliny the Younger wrote in one of his letters: "I scarcely ever miss a recitation. Of course, usually the people reciting are friends of mine; for there is almost no one who is fond of literary studies who is not also fond of me."

THE GAMES

The Romans referred to several different kinds of events as *ludi,* or games, including plays and other theatrical presentations. Plays were modeled on Greek comedies and tragedies, and only men acted in them. Pantomimes were more popular but also less respectable because they included female performers and appealed to the senses with music, dance, beautiful costumes and scenery, and lively action. Pantomimes may have been a little like ballets, since the performers acted out stories—usually based on familiar myths and legends—without using words. Quintilian wrote about how skilled and expressive the performers could be: "Their hands demand and promise, they summon and dismiss; they translate horror, fear, joy, sorrow. . . . They excite and they calm. They implore and they approve. They possess a power of imitation which replaces words."

Rome's oldest and most beloved form of popular entertainment was chariot racing. Races were held on a narrow oval track in an oblong roofless building called a circus. By the end of the second century there were eight circuses in and around the city of Rome alone; the largest of these, the Circus Maximus, had room for 250,000 spectators. In cities throughout the empire, chariot racing was highly organized. There were four racing factions, or teams,

named after the colors of their uniforms: Greens, Blues, Reds, and Whites. The same four colors were used wherever there was a circus, even though, for example, the Greens in Rome had a different owner and drivers than the Greens in Pompeii. The faction owners owned not only the chariots, horses, and stables, but also most of the drivers. Every faction had die-hard fans who sat together in the circus to cheer for their team and boo against the other factions. Sometimes fans of different factions even got into fistfights during a race.

Chariot racing was an exciting sport. The course was long and narrow, with tight lefthand turns at each end. The lightweight chariots, made of wicker or wood, might be pulled by two to ten horses, although most races were for four-horse chariots. The drivers used whips to urge their horses through seven laps around the track. (In the Circus Maximus, this made for a race of about 2.5 miles.) Crashes, injuries, and even deaths among both horses and drivers were common—but for the spectators, this element of danger only added to the excitement.

The excitement of a chariot race in the Circus Maximus is brought to life by a modern artist.

REST AND RECREATION

63

A CELEBRITY

Imperial Rome didn't have movie stars or rock stars, but it did have sports stars. Successful gladiators and charioteers became wildly popular celebrities. Although they were usually slaves or freedmen, they were admired by people at all levels of society. Wealthy fans—including some emperors—showered their favorites with gifts and invited them to fancy dinner parties and other social events.

Part of what made these stars of the arena and racetrack seem so glamorous, their lives so thrilling, was the danger involved in their professions. Every time a gladiator or chariot driver won a fight or a race, he was victorious not only over his opponents but also over death. Toward the end of the first century, a driver named Scorpus was one of the biggest stars ever, having won 2,048 races. But his good fortune couldn't last: at the age of twenty-six, he was killed in a crash on the racetrack. The poet Martial wrote this epitaph for him:

Here I lie, Scorpus, the pride of the noisy Circus, the darling of Rome, wildly cheered, but short-lived. Spiteful Lachesis* snatched me away in my twenty-sixth year. She counted my victories, not my years, and decided that I was an old man.

Alas, what a crime! You were cheated of your youth, Scorpus. You have fallen and died. Too soon have you harnessed the dark horses of death. Why did the finish line of the race, which you time and again hastened to cross, quickly covering the distance in your chariot, now become the finish of your life?

*the goddess who decided the length of a person's life

This detail from a mosaic shows a wild-animal fight in an amphitheater, with a gladiator killing a leopard.

Even bloodier games took place in the empire's amphitheaters. These nearly circular open-air stadiums were the scenes of gladiator combats and wild-animal fights. Gladiators were usually slaves or prisoners of war.* They were trained to fight in specific styles; for example, a *retiarius* was a gladiator who fought with a net and trident, while a Thracian used a curved sword and round shield. Most fights were not necessarily to the death, although a gladiator certainly could be killed or mortally injured during the course of combat. On the other hand, amphitheater shows also included executions, in which condemned criminals were sent to fight gladiators or wild animals. Those who received this sentence went into the arena unarmed, and they did not come out alive.

One of the world's most famous buildings, the Colosseum in Rome, was an amphitheater. When the emperor Titus opened it in 80 C.E., he sponsored one hundred days of elaborate spectacles, as reported by the senator and historian Dio Cassius:

> There was a battle between cranes and also between four elephants; animals both tame and wild were slain to the number of nine thousand; and women (not those of any

*Once in a while a freeborn man who could find no other work would become a gladiator. Also, some slaves who were freed after several years as gladiators continued to fight in the arena, charging high fees for doing so.

prominence, however) took part in despatching them. As for the men, several fought in single combat and several groups contended together both in infantry and naval battles. For Titus suddenly filled this same theatre with water and brought in horses and bulls and some other domesticated animals that had been taught to behave in the liquid element just as on land. He also brought in people on ships, who engaged in a sea-fight there.

Not all Romans enjoyed these types of events. Seneca the Younger, for one, was highly critical of their influence. He wrote to a friend, "There is nothing more harmful to one's character than attendance at some spectacle, because vices more easily creep into your soul while you are being entertained. When I return home from some spectacle, I am greedier, more aggressive . . . I am more cruel and inhumane. . . ." Most people today would agree with Seneca—but for a great many ancient Romans, it seems that amphitheater events gave them a welcome escape from their own poverty and powerlessness.

·VIII·

SURVIVING IN THE CITY

IF THERE COULD BE SOME WAY OF STOPPING HOUSES IN ROME
CATCHING FIRE THE WHOLE TIME, I SHOULD CERTAINLY SELL ALL MY
PROPERTY IN THE COUNTRY AND BUY URBAN PROPERTY.
—AULUS GELLIUS, *ATTIC NIGHTS*

Roman city could be a difficult and even dangerous place to live. Crime, crowding, noise, pollution, poverty, unemployment—cities everywhere have suffered from such problems. In the ancient world, some of these troubles were especially bad. For example, with no streetlights of any kind, it was very easy for thieves to sneak up on pedestrians at night. Not surprisingly, Roman city dwellers rarely went out after dark; if they had to, slaves or hired boys carried torches to light the way. Nighttime travelers who were poor rarely had these options. And thieves were not the only hazard, since it was difficult for people to even see where they were going in the darkness.

Along with kitchen garbage and other trash, urban pollution included sewage and animal manure. These wastes accumulated in

Apothecaries' shops, like this one in Rome, sold various medicinal substances, only some of which were effective.

alleyway cesspits and dung heaps, posing a constant threat to public health—and a persistent assault to the nose. While Rome and many other cities did have wonderful sewer systems for the time, the sewers mainly drained bathhouses and public lavatories, and they emptied the wastewater and untreated sewage into the nearest river.

The water system, excellent as it was coming from the countryside, also posed a danger; since lead pipes were frequently used, it is likely that a great number of Roman city dwellers suffered from lead poisoning. Lead was also an ingredient in some women's cosmetics—even makeup had its perils. Many Romans, however, did realize that lead was harmful; Vitruvius wrote, "water ought by no means to be conducted in lead pipes, if we want to have it wholesome." Unfortunately, Vitruvius's advice was largely ignored.

Disease was inescapable for rich and poor alike, although the poor were especially susceptible to illnesses caused by malnutrition and poor sanitation. But even for the wealthy, there were no vaccines, antibiotics, or advanced surgical procedures. There were also no standards of education for doctors. Good ones learned their profession by apprenticing to skilled physicians. Anyone, however, could claim to be a doctor, without any training at all. The most experienced doctors were still unable to cure a great number of illnesses. The average life expectancy for ancient Romans was only twenty-seven years.

⟡ THE ANNOYING SIDE ⟡ OF CITY LIFE

Juvenal may have come from a city about eighty miles southeast of Rome. After serving a term as *duovir* in his hometown, he moved to the capital, where he lived through many personal and political ups and downs. Between the years 110 and 127, he wrote his sixteen *Satires*, poems that exaggerated and ridiculed the annoyances and follies he witnessed every day in Rome. Here is a selection from Juvenal's third *Satire,* in which he complains about the noise and crowds that sometimes made city life nearly unbearable:

> Most sick men here die from insomnia (of course
> their illness starts with food undigested, clogging
> the burning stomach)—for in any rented room
> rest is impossible. It costs money to sleep in Rome.
> There is the root of the sickness. The movement of heavy waggons
> through narrow streets, the oaths of stalled cattle-drovers
> would break the sleep of a deaf man or a lazy walrus.
> On a morning call the crowd gives way before the passage
> of a millionaire carried above their heads in a litter,
> reading the while he goes, or writing, or sleeping unseen:
> for a man becomes sleepy with closed windows and comfort.
> Yet he'll arrive before us. We have to fight our way
> through a wave in front, and behind we are pressed by a huge mob
> shoving our hips; an elbow hits us here and a pole
> there, now we are smashed by a beam, now biffed by a barrel.
> Our legs are thick with mud, our feet are crushed by large
> ubiquitous shoes, a soldier's hobnail rests on our toe. . . .

CATASTROPHE!

Cities, with their crowded conditions, were highly vulnerable to epidemics and other disasters. One of the calamities most feared by city dwellers was fire. Spreading easily from building to building, a fire could wipe out whole neighborhoods in a very short time. Rome itself suffered several catastrophic fires. The worst one occurred in 64 C.E., during the reign of the emperor Nero. Tacitus described it:

> The blaze in its fury ran first through the level portions of the city, then rising to the hills, while it again devastated every place below them, it outstripped all preventive measures. . . . At last, after five days, an end was put to the conflagration . . . by the destruction of all buildings on a vast space, so that the violence of the fire was met by clear ground and an open sky. But before people laid aside their fears, the flames returned, with no less fury this second time. . . . Rome, indeed, is divided into fourteen districts, four of which remained uninjured, three were leveled to the ground, while in the other seven were left only a few shattered, half-burnt relics of houses.

Natural disasters also struck Roman cities from time to time. Early in the first century, the city of Sardis in Asia Minor was hit by a huge earthquake. The rebuilding of Sardis took more than a century. An earthquake that struck Pompeii in 62 did so much damage that some people thought this city should just be abandoned. It wasn't, and seventeen years later Pompeii and the neighboring town of Herculaneum were the victims of one of history's most famous disasters, the eruption of Mount Vesuvius. Both cities were buried under deep layers of volcanic debris. The catastrophe, however, preserved the two towns in an almost untouched state. Since the eighteenth century, archaeologists have been carefully unearthing and studying them, revealing ever more information about urban life in the Roman Empire.

REDUCING THE RISKS

Emperors sent relief money and gave other assistance to cities hit by disaster. For example, after the earthquake in Sardis, the emperor Tiberius pledged a huge sum of money for rebuilding and cancelled the Sardians' tax payments for five years. The emperor Titus arranged housing and financial help for many of the people who

The ruins of the Forum of Trajan in Rome. The slightly curved structure toward the back is all that remains of Trajan's Market. Even where there were no fires or natural disasters, time has taken its toll on the cities of the Roman Empire.

A cast of one of the victims of Vesuvius, which looms in the background

❧ EYEWITNESS TO DISASTER ❧

Pliny the Elder, admiral and famous scholar, commanded the Roman fleet that was based about nineteen miles across the Bay of Naples from Pompeii. His seventeen-year-old nephew, Pliny the Younger, was visiting him when Vesuvius erupted. Later Pliny the Younger wrote an eyewitness account of the disaster, beginning, "On 24 August, in the early afternoon, my mother drew his [Pliny the Elder's] attention to a cloud of unusual size. . . . Its general appearance . . . [was] like an umbrella pine, for it rose to a great height on a sort of trunk and then split off into branches. . . . Sometimes it looked white, sometimes blotched and dirty."

The admiral's scientific curiosity was awakened, and he set sail across the bay for a closer look. The expedition turned into a rescue mission, with several ships working to carry people away from the catastrophic eruption. "And now cinders, which grew thicker and hotter the nearer he approached, fell into the ships, then pumice stones, too, with stones blackened, scorched, and cracked by fire. Then the sea ebbed suddenly from under them, while the shore was blocked by landslips from the mountains."

Pliny the Elder commanded his ship to land about four miles south of Pompeii. Unable to put to sea again because of fierce wind and waves, he took refuge for the night in a friend's villa. By early morning, "the courtyard giving access to his room was full of ashes mixed with pumice stones, so that its level had risen, and if he had stayed in the room any longer, he would never have got out. The buildings were now shaking with violent shocks, and seemed to be swaying to and fro, as if they were torn from their foundations." Back at the naval base, Pliny the Younger and his mother experienced these same tremors and fled their house:

> The coaches that we had ordered out, though upon the most level ground, were sliding to and fro and could not be kept steady. . . . Then we beheld the sea sucked back, leaving many sea animals captive on the dry sand. . . . A black and dreadful cloud bursting out in gusts of igneous serpentine vapor now and again yawned open to reveal long, fantastic flames, resembling flashes of lightning but much larger. Soon afterward, the cloud began to descend upon the earth and cover the sea. Ashes now fell upon us, though as yet in no great quantity. I looked behind me; darkness came rolling over the land after us like a torrent. I proposed, while we yet could see, to turn aside, lest we should be knocked down in the road by a crowd that followed us, and trampled to death in the dark. We had scarce sat down when darkness overspread us. . . . You could hear the shrieks of women and crying children and the shouts of men; some were seeking their children, others their parents; some praying to die, from the very fear of dying; many lifting their hands to the gods; but the greater part imagining that there were no gods left anywhere, that the last and eternal night was come upon the world.

This cloud of ash and poisonous gas thinned out as it crossed the bay, and so Pliny the Younger lived to tell the tale. His uncle was not so lucky. He had left the villa and gone to the shore to see if there was any way to escape. Surrounded by the dark cloud from the volcano, choking on the sulfurous fumes, Pliny the Elder collapsed on the beach and died, one of Vesuvius's thousands of victims.

fled their homes when Vesuvius began to erupt. Other emperors, too, looked for various ways to improve life in the empire's cities.

For the city of Rome, Augustus established not only the police force-like urban cohort but also the *vigiles*. These were night watchmen and, more importantly, trained firefighters. There were 3,500 (later increased to 7,000) men in the *vigiles*, and some of them also did duty in Ostia, the port city that served Rome. The commander of the *vigiles* was an equestrian, but the firefighters themselves were freedmen.

The great fire of 64 showed that some blazes were too huge even for the *vigiles* to handle, so Nero decreed new fire safety regulations. These included limiting the height of apartment buildings, requiring fireproof stone to be used in a large part of all new construction, leaving more open space in front of buildings, and keeping firefighting equipment available in the courtyards of all residences. Many other cities followed Rome's model in setting up fire-safety laws and firefighting units.

Another urban problem that demanded attention was poverty. The patron-client relationship was a kind of welfare system, since patrons' gifts of food and money helped many of the working poor as well as the unemployed. But too often this was not enough. Many poor citizens relied on a monthly distribution of free grain by the government. The emperors did their best to help assure the timely delivery of large amounts of grain to Rome—there was always a danger of riots if the supply ran low. As an additional measure to keep the populace happy, emperors occasionally handed out gifts of money, food, and clothes.

In the second century the emperor Trajan established a welfare program specifically to help poor children. Every year a sum of money was distributed to various Italian cities for the benefit of these children. Many other wealthy Romans also set up charitable funds, like a man from North Africa who gave his city a large amount of money so that "there may be fed and maintained each year 300 boys and 300 girls." Among other charitable acts, Pliny the Younger donated funds to his hometown in northern Italy to support poor children and to establish a school, a library, and a bathhouse. Pliny and those like him felt that since they were fortunate enough to be wealthy and educated, it was their duty to use at least some of their resources for the public good.

This attitude toward charity and public service is one of the great legacies of the Roman Empire. Looking back, we may be able to learn from the Romans how to solve some of the problems that confront our cities and our society today. Sometimes the history of the empire shows us possible solutions; at other times it warns us what to avoid. The Romans laid much of the foundation for our modern city-based lifestyle. To know their story is to know ourselves all the better.

GLOSSARY

amphitheater an oval, nearly circular, stadium, mainly for shows involving combat or wild-animal fights

aqueduct an artificial channel to carry water from its source to a city

arena an amphitheater's central, ground-level area, where the spectacles took place

atrium the front room of a Roman house, used to receive visitors

basilica a large rectangular building used for public meetings, law courts, and government offices. In a private home, a basilica was a rectangular meeting room.

circus a long, oval stadium where chariot races were held; a racetrack

equestrians members of Rome's second highest class, ranking below senators. In general, they were wealthy businessmen. *Equestrians* comes from *equites,* which literally means "horsemen" or "knights," because in early Roman times these were the men wealthy enough to afford warhorses and equipment for fighting on horseback.

eulogy a speech given at a funeral to praise the dead person. Upper-class Romans often delivered eulogies in the forum and then had them inscribed on marble.

forum the civic center and main meeting place of a Roman city, with

government buildings, offices, shops, and temples surrounding a large open area. In Rome itself there were six forums: the ancient original Forum, and additional forums built by Julius Caesar and by the emperors Augustus, Nerva, Vespasian, and Trajan.

fresco a wall painting made on fresh plaster

gladiator a professional fighter (nearly always a slave) trained for combat in the amphitheater

infantry a body of soldiers who fight on foot

legion a unit of the Roman army, made up of about five thousand men

mosaic a picture or design made from small square pieces of stone that were either dyed or, in the best-quality mosaics, chosen for their natural colors

orator a person skilled in writing and making speeches

pantomime a ballet-like performance in which dancers, accompanied by music, wordlessly acted out stories from myth or legend. The performers were usually slaves and included women as well as men.

peristyle a courtyard surrounded by a covered walkway

tablinum the office or study of the head of the household

trident a three-pronged spear

FOR FURTHER READING

Amery, Heather, and Patricia Vanags. *Rome & Romans.* London: Usborne, 1997.

Biesty, Stephen. *Rome in Spectacular Cross-Section.* New York: Scholastic Nonfiction, 2003.

Corbishley, Mike. *What Do We Know about the Romans?* New York: Peter Bedrick Books, 1991.

Denti, Mario. *Journey to the Past: Imperial Rome.* Austin, TX and New York: Raintree Steck-Vaughn, 2001.

Ganeri, Anita. *How Would You Survive as an Ancient Roman?* New York: Franklin Watts, 1995.

Hart, Avery, and Sandra Gallagher. *Ancient Rome! Exploring the Culture, People and Ideas of This Powerful Empire.* Charlotte, VT: Williamson Publishing, 2002.

Hinds, Kathryn. *The Ancient Romans.* New York: Benchmark Books, 1997.

Hodge, Susie. *Ancient Roman Art.* Chicago: Heinemann Library, 1998.

Jovinelly, Joann, and Jason Netelkos. *The Crafts and Culture of the Romans.* New York: Rosen Publishing Group, 2002.

Macaulay, David. *City: A Story of Roman Planning and Construction.* Boston: Houghton Mifflin, 1974.

Macdonald, Fiona. *The Roman Colosseum.* New York: Peter Bedrick Books, 1996.

———. *Women in Ancient Rome.* New York: Peter Bedrick Books, 2000.

Mann, Elizabeth. *The Roman Colosseum.* New York: Mikaya Press, 1998.

Nardo, Don. *Life in Ancient Rome.* San Diego: Lucent Books, 1997.

———. *Life of a Roman Soldier.* San Diego: Lucent Books, 2001.

———. *The Roman Empire.* San Diego: Lucent Books, 1994.

Seely, John, and Elizabeth Seely. *Pompeii and Herculaneum.* Chicago: Heinemann Library, 2000.

Tanaka, Shelley. *The Buried City of Pompeii: What It Was Like When Vesuvius Exploded.* Toronto: Madison Press Books, 1997.

Whittock, Martyn. *The Colosseum and the Roman Forum.* Chicago: Heinemann
Library, 2003.

ONLINE INFORMATION*

Ancient Rome.

    http://www.mce.k12tn.net/ancient_rome/rome.htm

Carr, Karen E. *History for Kids: Ancient Rome.*

    http://www.historyforkids.org/learn/romans/index.htm

Goldberg, Dr. Neil. *The Rome Project.*

    http://www.dalton.org/groups/rome/index.html

Illustrated History of the Roman Empire.

    http://www.roman-empire.net/

Michael C. Carlos Museum of Emory University. *Odyssey Online: Rome.*

    http://carlos.emory.edu/ODYSSEY/ROME/homepg.html

Nova Online. *Secrets of Lost Empires: Roman Bath.*

    http://www.pbs.org/wgbh/nova/lostempires/roman

The Roman Empire in the First Century.

    http://www.pbs.org/empires/romans

Secrets of the Dead: The Great Fire of Rome.

    http://www.pbs.org/wnet/secrets/case_rome/index.html

Thayer, Bill. *Lacus Curtius: Into the Roman World.*

    http://www.ukans.edu/history/index/europe/ancient_rome/E/ Roman/home.html

*All Internet sites were available and accurate when this book was sent to press.

BIBLIOGRAPHY

Adkins, Lesley, and Roy A. Adkins. *Handbook to Life in Ancient Rome.* New
York: Oxford University Press, 1994.

Boardman, John, et al., editors. *The Oxford Illustrated History of the Roman
World.* Oxford: Oxford University Press, 1988.

Carcopino, Jerome. *Daily Life in Ancient Rome.* Ed. Henry T. Rowell. Trans. E. O. Lorimer. New Haven, CT: Yale University Press, 1968.

Editors of Time-Life Books. *Pompeii: The Vanished City.* Alexandria, VA: Time-Life Books, 1992.

Editors of Time-Life Books. *Rome: Echoes of Imperial Glory.* Alexandria, VA: Time-Life Books, 1994.

Edwards, John. *Roman Cookery: Elegant & Easy Recipes from History's First Gourmet,* rev. ed. Point Roberts, WA: Hartley & Marks, 1986.

Fantham, Elaine, et al. *Women in the Classical World: Image and Text.* New York: Oxford University Press, 1994.

Grabsky, Phil. *I, Caesar: Ruling the Roman Empire.* London: BBC Books, 1997.

Highet, Gilbert. *Poets in a Landscape.* New York: Alfred A. Knopf, 1957.

Mellor, Ronald, ed. *The Historians of Ancient Rome: An Anthology of the Major Writings.* New York: Routledge, 1998.

Santosuosso, Antonio. *Storming the Heavens: Soldiers, Emperors, and Civilians in the Roman Empire.* Boulder, CO: Westview Press, 2001.

Scarre, Chris. *Chronicle of the Roman Emperors: The Reign-by-Reign Record of the Rulers of Imperial Rome.* London: Thames & Hudson, 1995.

Shelton, Jo-Ann. *As the Romans Did: A Source Book in Roman Social History,* 2nd ed. New York: Oxford University Press, 1998.

Vitruvius. *The Ten Books on Architecture.* Trans. Morris Hicky Morgan. New York: Dover Publications, 1960.

Wells, Colin. *The Roman Empire,* 2nd ed. Cambridge, MA: Harvard University Press, 1992.

Zanker, Paul. *Pompeii: Public and Private Life.* Trans. Deborah Lucas Schneider. Cambridge, MA: Harvard University Press, 1998.

SOURCES FOR QUOTATIONS

Chapter I

p. 1 "Even now": author's translation of Ovid's *Metamorphoses,* Book
XV, lines 444–445. original Latin text at:
http://www.thelatinlibrary.com/ovid/ovid.met15.shtml

p. 2 "Goddess of continents": Carcopino, *Daily Life in Ancient Rome,* p. 21.

p. 4 "Will anybody": Editors of Time-Life, *Rome: Echoes of Imperial Glory,*
p. 154.

p. 5 "the charms," "Agricola gave": Mellor, *The Historians of Ancient
Rome,* p. 404.

p. 7 "I used to": Boardman, *The Oxford Illustrated History of the Roman
World,* p. 208.

Chapter II

p. 10 "the Roman people": Vitruvius, *The Ten Books on Architecture,* p. 57.

p. 13 "an admirably large": Grabsky, *I, Caesar,* p. 25.

p. 16 "We inhabit": Carcopino, *Daily Life in Ancient Rome,* p. 32.

p. 18 "because I saw": Vitruvius, *The Ten Books on Architecture,* p. 4.

p. 19 "to suit" and "Men of everyday": ibid., p. 182.

p. 21 "that perfection": ibid., p. 14.

Chapter III

p. 23 "Hello Profit": Shelton, *As the Romans Did,* p. 135.

p. 26 "You cannot control": ibid., p. 176.

p. 26 "I was happy": ibid., pp. 182–183.

p. 28 "The muleteers": Wells, *The Roman Empire,* p. 41.

p. 30 "Grammarian, orator": Boardman, *The Oxford Illustrated History of
the Roman World,* p. 341.

p. 30 "Fortune, do you": Shelton, *As the Romans Did,* p. 195.

p. 30 "I hope that": ibid:, p. 194.

Chapter IV

p. 33 "If you ask": Shelton, *As the Romans Did,* p. 148.

p. 35 "Once upon": ibid., p. 13.

p. 35 "This morning": Carcopino, *Daily Life in Ancient Rome,* p. 172.

p. 35 "How many": Shelton, *As the Romans Did,* pp. 14–15.

p. 37 "to wear the toga": Mellor, *The Historians of Ancient Rome,* p. 507.

p. 38 "Your teeth": Boardman, *The Oxford Illustrated History of the Roman World,* p. 165.

p. 39 "Then they march": Shelton, *As the Romans Did,* p. 254.

p. 41 "It is chiefly": Mellor, *The Historians of Ancient Rome,* p. 446.

Chapter V

p. 43 "Guardians are appointed": Shelton, *As the Romans Did,* p. 34.

p. 44 "Don't marry": ibid., p. 299.

p. 45 "My dearest mother": Fantham, *Women in the Classical World,* p. 318.

p. 48 "My hateful birthday": ibid., p. 324.

p. 49 "She says that after": ibid., p. 368.

Chapter VI

p. 51 "Praise lifts": Shelton, *As the Romans Did,* p. 31.

p. 52 "If I receive": ibid., p. 28.

p. 54 "Let his lessons": ibid., p. 102.

p. 55 "Viccentia, sweetest": Fantham, *Women in the Classical World,* p. 377.

p. 56 "My father": Shelton, *As the Romans Did,* p. 18.

Chapter VII

p. 59 "Hunting, bathing": Editors of Time-Life, *Rome: Echoes of Imperial Glory,* p. 117.

p. 62 "I scarcely ever": Shelton, *As the Romans Did,* p. 319.

p. 62 "Their hands": Carcopino, *Daily Life in Ancient Rome,* p. 227.

p. 64 "Here I lie": Shelton, *As the Romans Did,* p. 346.

p. 65 "There was a battle": Scarre, *Chronicle of the Roman Emperors,* p. 73.

p. 66 "There is nothing": Shelton, *As the Romans Did,* p. 355.

Chapter VIII

p. 67 "If there could": Wells, *The Roman Empire,* p. 196.

p. 68 "water ought": Vitruvius, *The Ten Books on Architecture,* p. 247.

p. 69 "Most sick men": Highet, *Poets in a Landscape,* pp. 221–222.

p. 70 "The blaze": Mellor, *The Historians of Ancient Rome,* pp. 471–472.

p. 72 "On 24 August": Wells, *The Roman Empire,* p. 188.

p. 72 "And now cinders": Editors of Time-Life, *Pompeii: The Vanished City,* p. 20.

p. 73 "the courtyard": Wells, *The Roman Empire,* p. 188.

p. 73 "The coaches": Editors of Time-Life, *Pompeii: The Vanished City,* p. 23.

p. 75 "there may be fed": Shelton, *As the Romans Did,* p. 36.

INDEX

THE CITY

ABOUT THE AUTHOR

KATHRYN HINDS grew up near Rochester, New York. In college she studied music and writing, and went on to do graduate work in comparative literature and medieval studies at the City University of New York. She has written a number of books for young people, including Benchmark Books' LIFE IN THE MIDDLE AGES series and LIFE IN THE RENAISSANCE series. Kathryn now lives in Georgia's Blue Ridge Mountains with her husband, their son, two dogs, and three cats. When she is not writing, she enjoys dancing, reading, playing music, gardening, and taking walks in the woods.

FOX GRADIN, CELESTIAL STUDIOS PHOTOGRAPHY